Christian Hardinghaus

The Key to Mulholland Drive

Understanding David Lynch

2

IMPRINT

Copyright © 2025 Christian Hardinghaus

Picture credits: All film stills used were taken from: David Lynch, Mulholland Drive 2001, produced by Pierre Edelman, Alain Sarde. © Concorde. All rights reserved.

Table of Contents

FOR DAVID LYNCH: AN OBITUARY AND FOREWORD TO THE NEW EDITION 6

MINDFUCK: CONFUSION WITH A CONCEPT 10

UNDERSTANDING MULHOLLAND DRIVE AND LYNCH 13

    THOUSANDS OF POSSIBLE INTERPRETATIONS 14

    AS TOLD BY CULT DIRECTOR DAVID LYNCH 17

THE DECRYPTION CODE: THE STORY OF MULHOLLAND DRIVE 22

    TEN CLUES FROM DAVID LYNCH 23

    UNDERSTANDING MULHOLLAND DRIVE: THE CHRONOLOGY OF EVENTS 24

    THE LIFE OF DIANE SELWYN: WHAT HAPPENED? 28

PLAY OF A DREAMER: A STEP-BY-STEP ANALYSIS OF MULHOLLAND DRIVE 43

    A contract killing in a restaurant 44

    FROM THE DANCE INTO THE WILD DREAM 46

    A MONSTER BEHIND WINKIE'S 49

    THE BIRTH OF BETTY ELMS - AND HOW CAMILLA BECOMES RITA 52

    A BOTCHED CASTING AND A SAD DIRECTOR 59

REVERSED ROLES: A DREAM POOL PARTY .65

HIDDEN CLUES: DIANE'S CHILD ABUSE AND HER RED LIGHT ACTIVITY 77

COLOR AND NUMBER GAMES 84

AN EERILY ROMANTIC ENDING 95

PANDORA'S BOX 101

A WACKY SHOOT BEHIND A WACKY STORY 104

REFERENCES IN AND CURIOSITIES ABOUT MULHOLLAND DRIVE 110

PRODUCTION NOTES 128

FILMOGRAPHY 136

FOR DAVID LYNCH: AN OBITUARY AND FOREWORD TO THE NEW EDITION

David Lynch's death on January 15, 2025, in Los Angeles has deprived the world of an irreplaceable voice of surreal poetry. The director succumbed to incurable emphysema at the age of 78. He was artistically active until the end and had numerous projects planned, including new films, musical compositions, and a sequel to his cult series, my favorite series, *Twin Peaks*. His death leaves a huge gap in the film and art world, but like his characters, his work lives on - as a hall of mirrors of dream and reality that forces us to dig deeper, look closer, and find the beauty in the inexplicable.

Lynch, the painter of the unconscious, has shown me as a writer that the greatest truths often lie in the twilight. My exploration of his work began in the lecture halls of my film studies, which I completed in 2007. Back then, I focused on the phenomenon of the "mindfuck" in cinema - that moment when reality dissolves and the audience is plunged into the unknown. *Mulholland Drive* was the ultimate lesson for me. After my master's degree, I published my first analysis of the film. In 2014, I developed the ideas into a book, which I now wish to publish in a new edition - refined in terms of language, expanded in terms of content, and featuring many additional references.

Lynch's love of the enigmatic was never a mere provocation. It was an invitation to understand the world as a collage of contradictions. The director, who showed "both the glitter and the dirt under the Hollywood carpet", shaped my approach to historical material: truth and myth are also superimposed in stories about the past. Lynch's advice, "Keep your eye on the donut, not on the hole," reminds me that even in the bleakest stories of the Second World War, which my non-fiction and historical novels mainly deal with, there must be a glimmer of hope.

"Would Lynch like it?" - That's the question I ask myself when I create a plot twist that breaks up reality. I hide little "mindfuck elements" in every one of my thrillers and historical novels. Lynch, who revered Kafka and dissolved the boundaries of identity in *Mulholland Drive*, would probably have smiled at my attempts to surprise readers with surreal moments in historical war scenarios. Lynch's death is not an ending, but a transition, like the leap through the blue box in *Mulholland Drive*. It is a central symbol of the film, serving as a metaphor between different levels of reality and a key to insight.

In his spirit, I dedicate this new edition not only to him but to all those who are prepared to lose themselves in the thicket of the imagination. Because, as he said, "*Absurdity is what I like most in life.*" May his dreams continue to haunt our stories, challenging, unsettling, and enchanting us. "*It's a beautiful day with golden sunshine and blue skies all the way.*"

Thank you, David. For the questions without answers, the dreams without alarm clocks, and the many cups of black coffee I've drunk since Twin Peaks.
Christian Hardinghaus in February 2025.

MINDFUCK: CONFUSION WITH A CONCEPT

Imagine this: You suddenly realize that you've been dead for a week and only talk to ghosts. Or that your marriage, your partner, your life together - none of it was ever real. Perhaps you realize that you are schizophrenic and lead a double life: a loving family man by day, a serial killer by night. Or you know that the dog you feed every day is long dead and rotting in your kitchen. The world as you know it ended a long time ago.

This unsettling feeling that everything you thought was true is suddenly being called into question is called "mindfuck". A term originating from the film industry that is difficult to translate into German. It is somewhere between "simulated reality" and "mindfuck" - but the effect is more important than the translation: an effect that makes us doubt our senses and reality.

The highlight of every mindfuck work lies in the staging. The director plays a clever trick on us, sending us on an unexpected and often disturbing journey. Typical of the mindfuck film is a surprising twist shortly before the end. The viewer initially feels deceived before realizing the connections, and it is precisely then that the filmmaker has achieved his goal. What is special about this is that not only the audience but also the protagonist is overwhelmed by the revelation. Unlike in a thriller, where the perpetrator knows his secret, here the truth comes as a shock to everyone involved.

When the director finally clarifies the situation, certain scenes turn out to be illusions, mirages, or hallucinations. Flashbacks reveal new perspectives, and the viewer needs time to understand everything. Many rewind and watch the movie again - this effect is intentional.

The mindfuck director often scatters subtle

clues that only make sense on the second or third viewing. The attraction lies in the subsequent realization. However, the key is to provide sufficient clues to make the resolution credible. The cleverer the clues, the more ingenious the work.

However, some mindfuck films do without a clear explanation and leave the interpretation up to the viewer. The director remains silent, only hinting instead of explaining. The film becomes a puzzle that triggers years of discussion - a technique that directors like David Lynch, in particular, have mastered.

UNDERSTANDING MULHOLLAND DRIVE AND LYNCH

Not yet immersed in *Mulholland Drive*? Then you'd better put this decoding aside! Experience David Lynch's masterpiece with an open mind - without prior knowledge, without explanations. Return afterwards - with open eyes and an open mind.

Have you already seen *Mulholland Drive*? Fascinated but confused? Welcome! But beware: this book does not provide simple answers. To decipher the puzzle, the movie should still be fresh in your memory. My advice: watch it again - preferably immediately.

You have absorbed the images, the music, the atmosphere. You were frightened by the monster behind Winkie's, suffered with Diane and felt the tension in Club Silencio. But what does it all mean? What is real, what is illusion? And what secrets does the blue box hold? Do you already have a theory? Great!

This book is your key to *Mulholland Drive*. It invites you to unravel the mysteries, discover new connections and look at the movie from a completely new perspective.

THOUSANDS OF POSSIBLE INTERPRETATIONS

Mulholland Drive - one movie, countless interpretations. Fans have been puzzling over the meaning of David Lynch's masterpiece for almost 25 years. Dream, drug intoxication, parallel universe - the theories are as varied as the fan community. A definitive answer? There isn't one.

Lynch deliberately avoids clear explanations and leaves many storylines open. In doing so, he challenges the audience to draw their own conclusions and interpret the film on different levels. *Mulholland Drive* is more than just a story - it is a cinematic experience that pushes the boundaries of the medium and goes far beyond conventional storytelling.

My interpretation, which I present to you here, serves as a starting point for your consideration. It is based on well-founded arguments and my personal perspective. But ultimately, it is up to you to find your own truth in this puzzle.

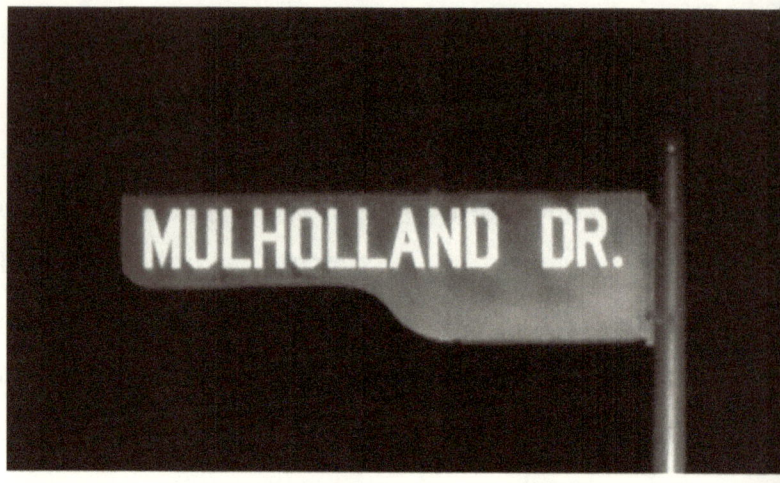

MULHOLLAND DR - Dream Road in the Darkness

AS TOLD BY CULT DIRECTOR DAVID LYNCH

What makes *Mulholland* Drive a cult film? First of all, its creator, David Keith Lynch, was born in Missoula, Montana, on January 20, 1946, the son of an agricultural scientist and an English teacher. His childhood in small American towns, characterized by frequent moves, seemed idyllic, but Lynch developed an early eye for the darkness beneath the surface. At the age of 14, he discovered his love of art, inspired by a fellow painter who was a friend of his father. After various art studies, he established himself as a visionary director in 1977 with his debut film *Eraserhead*.

Works such as *The Elephant Man*, *Blue Velvet,* and *Mulholland Drive* followed, earning him several Oscar nominations. Lynch's surrealist style, non-linear narratives, and unique visual language often blur the lines between dream and reality, exploring the dark side of the American dream, identity, and the subconscious. In addition to filmmaking, Lynch is also known as a visual artist, musician, and proponent of Transcendental Meditation. He has been married several times and has four children. As one of the most influential and innovative directors of his generation, he seamlessly combined the everyday with the surreal and delved into the psychological abysses.

A new Lynch film is more than just a trip to the movies; it is a surreal, mystical journey into the viewer's dreams and fears. Lynch's narratives are fragmented, non-linear, revolve around traumatic events and challenge the audience to put the pieces of the puzzle together themselves. Visually, he relies on expressive colors, unusual camera angles and often explores the dark abysses of the human psyche. He works intuitively and is guided by sudden ideas.

Lynch dispenses with classic story arcs and

happy endings. His films are full of detail, artfully staged, and full of symbolism and metaphors. His irrational, disturbing themes have a magical appeal that attracts cineastes. Lynch's cinema is eerie, bizarre, romantic, and postmodern. Actors, music, props - everything is meticulously selected. His films often have open endings, but these are revealed if you engage with his imagination and narrative structure.

Cult films are timeless, celebrated and loved across generations. They are not blockbusters, but captivate with their depth and artistic aspirations. Insider tips whose significance never fades. This applies to almost all of David Lynch's works. His *Twin Peaks* series is streamed worldwide. *Mulholland Drive* achieved a top rating of 7.9/10 on IMDB, and over 90,000 viewers gave the film the highest rating of 10. *Mulholland Drive* is cult!

In *Mulholland Drive*, Lynch unleashes a fireworks display of innovative narrative techniques that make the film a multi-layered and fascinating experience. He deliberately breaks with conventional narrative structures and presents the story in a non-linear, dream-like sequence that challenges the viewer to interpret it actively. Reality, dream and fantasy blur into one another and create a surreal, confusing atmosphere. Lynch makes masterful use of visual and auditory means: the chiaroscuro technique with its strong contrasts of light and dark creates an ominous mood, while the sophisticated sound design underlines the eerie atmosphere. He cleverly subverts the audience's expectations by playing with familiar Hollywood stereotypes and film noir elements, but deconstructs them as the film progresses. Metafictional elements, such as the famous Club Silencio scene, also address the artificiality of the film itself. Recurring symbols and visual motifs, such as keys, boxes, or blue objects, open up different levels of interpretation. The doubling of characters across varying levels of reality also contributes to the narrative's ambiguity.

22

THE DECRYPTION CODE: THE STORY OF MULHOLLAND DRIVE

David Lynch took the secrets of his films to his grave - or so it seems. But even his most complex works are not impenetrable. *Mulholland Drive* may seem confusing at first glance, but behind the façade, there may be a coherent, meaningful story waiting to be discovered.

Lynch himself left us ten clues to help us decipher *Mulholland Drive*. But beware: these clues are not a shortcut to instant enlightenment. They are pieces of a jigsaw puzzle that only reveal a complete picture with patience and attention.

Before I analyze Lynch's clues in detail, I invite you once again to embark on your search. Take the plunge into the labyrinth of *Mulholland Drive* and try to unravel the mystery.

TEN CLUES FROM DAVID LYNCH

1. Pay special attention to the beginning of the movie: Two important clues can be found even before the opening title.

2. Observe when and where red lampshades play a role.

3. Pay attention to the title of the movie for which Adam Kesher listens to and looks at actresses. Is this title repeated elsewhere?

4. An accident is a terrible event. Note the exact location of the accident.

5 Who gives whom a key - and why?

6 Pay close attention to the clothes, the ashtray, the cup of coffee.

7. What is felt, observed, and gained at Club Silencio?

8. Does Camilla's talent alone help her?

9. Observe closely the events surrounding the man behind Winkie's.

10. Where is Aunt Ruth?

UNDERSTANDING MULHOLLAND DRIVE: THE CHRONOLOGY OF EVENTS

Before we examine Lynch's clues, let's begin with the basics. David Lynch's narration is unreliable. This means that you cannot rely on what the characters say. Like the entire narrative style, they are shaped in such a way that they can mislead the audience. The biggest challenge in understanding *Mulholland Drive*, however, lies in its additional non-linear narrative style. The chronology of events in the movie deviates from the actual sequence of the plot. To add to the confusion, the story unfolds on three different levels, which we will now unravel.

The movie mainly takes place on the dream level. The reality level, on the other hand, is divided into two: the cinematic present and the cinematic past. The past is reconstructed through the memories of the protagonist Diane Selwyn (Naomi Watts). In her dreams, Diane transforms her self-image by processing and reinventing her memories through her alter ego, Betty Elms (also Naomi Watts).

To decipher Mulholland Drive, it is essential to assign a chronology of events to the respective narrative levels. The following table provides you with a detailed overview of all the film scenes in their original order and assigns them to the dream level, the present reality, or the remembered past.

Movie Section	Narrative Layer
WE SEE DIANE, WHO WON A DANCE COMPETITION. AN ELDERLY COUPLE IS HAPPY ABOUT HER SUCCESS. SHE BEAMS.	REMEMBERED PAST
FROM THE EGO PERSPECTIVE, WE HEAR DIANE BREATHING AND FALLING INTO HER BED.	PRESENT REALITY
DIANE BEGINS TO DREAM. HER DREAM IS THE STORY OF BETTY, RITA AND ADAM. IT STARTS WITH BETTY'S ARRIVAL AT LOS ANGELES AIRPORT AND ENDS WITH HER NEIGHBOR KNOCKING ON DIANE'S APARTMENT DOOR.	DREAM
DIANE WAKES UP AND OPENS THE APARTMENT DOOR. A BLUE KEY LIES ON THE TABLE. THE NEIGHBOR GETS SOME THINGS THAT BELONG TO HER. DIANE MAKES COFFEE AND SITS ON THE COUCH.	PRESENT REALITY

DIANE REMEMBERS THE PAST. WHAT HAPPENED BEFORE HER DREAM: HER EX-GIRLFRIEND CAMILLA ENDS THE RELATIONSHIP ON THE SOFA. SHE MASTURBATES DESPERATELY. CAMILLA FORCES HER TO WATCH AT A THEATER REHEARSAL HOW SHE KISSES ADAM. SHE IS INVITED TO A POOL PARTY AT ADAM'S. SHE HIRES THE KILLER AT WINKIE'S WHO IS SUPPOSED TO KILL CAMILLA.	REMEMBERED PAST
DIANE LOOKS AT THE BLUE KEY LYING ON HER TABLE. CAMILLA IS DEAD. SHE HALLUCINATES AN ELDERLY COUPLE EMERGING FROM UNDER THE THRESHOLD. SHE FLEES TO THE BEDROOM AND SHOOTS HERSELF.	PRESENT REALITY
FLASHBACK TO THE MONSTER, THE HAPPY DIANE, CLUB SILENCIO, THE BLUE-HAIRED WOMAN: SILENCIO!	PRESENT REALITY (DEATH EXPERIENCE)

THE LIFE OF DIANE SELWYN: WHAT HAPPENED?

To reconstruct Diane Selwyn's real life, we must relate the diverse information from the various narrative levels of the film. This is the only way we can present her story and the events in *Mulholland Drive* in a chronologically correct way. Our first goal is to organize the plot and identify the characters and their roles in reality.

In the "Play of a Dreamer" chapter, we will examine in detail the crucial clues that help reconstruct the story, even the most hidden ones. Pay attention to subtle hints and symbolism. Their interpretation may remain ambiguous, but they are crucial to the movie's impact.

Even if the reconstruction of the story may seem unusual at first, it should be accepted for the time being. Understanding the actual plot is crucial to comprehend the derivation and justification in the following chapter - in other words, why the story had to happen in one way or another.

Mulholland Drive tells the story of Diane Selwyn, who hails from the small town of Deep River, Ontario, Canada. In her early childhood, she had to endure sexual abuse by her father and the non-intervention of her mother. After both die in a car accident, 16-year-old Diane goes to live with her grandparents (Jeanne Bates, Dan Birnbaum). But even there, her everyday life is anything but happy: she only receives recognition from her grandparents through outstanding achievements.

To earn the love her parents have denied her, Diane tries to make her grandparents proud in various ways. She loves dancing and experiences her greatest success to date when, one day, she wins a jitterbug dance competition, a name given to an American swing dance style of the 1930s. For the first time, she receives the encouragement of her grandparents, who even approve of her career aspirations to become an actress.

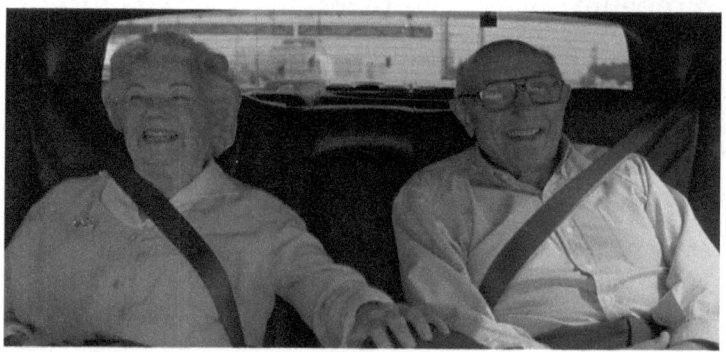

Grandparents with false pride

When her Aunt Ruth (Maya Bond), a casting agent in Hollywood, dies, Diane sees her chance to leave Canada and escape life with her grandparents. Aunt Ruth, who had hardly supported Diane before, apparently having little faith in her talent, nevertheless leaves her an opportunity to pursue her dream: In her estate, Ruth allows her niece to take over her apartment in Hollywood. It is located in the popular 1612 Havenhurst residential complex. Diane can live there as long as she pays the rent. Ruth also leaves her a letter with important contacts and some money to help her get started.

In Hollywood, Diane gets an audition at her aunt's casting agency, arranged by her aunt's friend Wally Brown (James Karen). They are looking for the leading actress for the *Sylvia North story*. Out of consideration for her recently deceased, influential aunt, Diane is initially certified as talented. However, she is only auditioning as a favor. She is not considered suitable for the role, and Diane is unable to change this impression.

The director, Bob Rooker (Wayne Grace), gives the role to Camilla Rhodes (Laura Elena Harring). Diane meets Camilla during rehearsals and is impressed by her acting skills. The two meet several times and become friends. Camilla gives Diane a few supporting roles in films, but she can't make a living from them, and a bigger acting job doesn't materialize.

Soon, Diane can no longer afford the rent for her aunt's apartment. She has to leave her aunt's apartment on Havenhurst Drive and move into a shabby park hotel. The owner of the hotel is called Cookie (Geno Silva). Even there, Diane has difficulty paying the rent without lucrative engagements. Cookie regularly visits her and demands his money. To make ends meet, Diane takes a job as a waitress at Winkie's, a fast-food restaurant. Although the money she earns is enough for a simple life, Diane still dreams of becoming a star and surrounds herself with wealthy people from the scene after work. She needs more money to finance a higher standard of living and gain recognition as an actress.

In desperation, Diane takes a job as a call girl and is registered in the "black book" of pimp Ed (Vincent Castellanos). Some of her clients disgust her, as they remind her of the abuse she suffered at the hands of her father. One of these clients is the rich producer Luigi Castigliane (Angelo Badalamenti). Diane puts up with the sex in the hope of getting an engagement in a movie.

However, Diane finds another rich film producer, Mr. Roque (Michael J. Anderson), so repulsive that she rejects him as a client, even though he is prepared to pay her pimp Ed more money than usual. Mr. Roque repeatedly attempts to contact her by telephone through intermediaries. Ed is annoyed, but is unable to convince Diane. Instead, he cuts her share of the income. Diane is now forced to work on the street behind the Pink's hot dog restaurant to earn money.

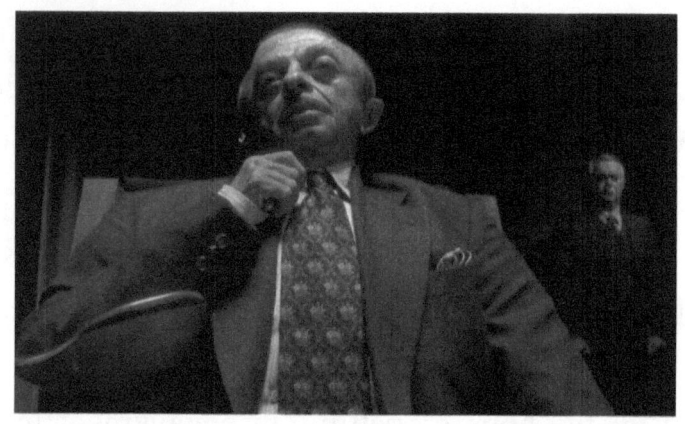

Mr. Roque harasses Diane over the phone.

Camilla can't live on her talent alone either. She also has to make sacrifices and "work her way up" in the film business. However, she has the necessary flair to make a career for herself. Camilla earns a little more money through her acting work and decides to move in with Diane. Their new home is apartment no. 12 in the Sierra

Bonita residential complex.

The two soon become close and begin a passionate romance. While Diane falls madly in love, for Camilla, it is only a brief affair. Camilla falls in love with the successful director Adam Kesher (Justin Theroux), in whose new film she gets a leading role and through whom she can hope for further offers. She moves out of the apartment they share, partly because she no longer wants to have anything to do with the red light district and feels that Diane's less prestigious side job is affecting her.

While Camilla achieves great success in Hollywood thanks to her relationship with Adam, Diane's life continues to deteriorate. There are problems on the street, and Mr. Roque still won't leave her alone. Joe (Mark Pellegrino), her pimp on the street, finds himself in strong competition with Ed, who provides Diane with wealthier clients. Through Diane, Joe discovers where and how Ed records his business: in a black book. Joe decides to kill Ed and steal this book from him to obtain the addresses of solvent clients whom he might be able to blackmail. He also eliminates his competitor.

Diane can no longer cope with all this, and above all with the separation from Camilla. She seeks help from the therapist, Herb, but he is unable to help her overcome her fears. Diane then decides to swap apartments in the Sierra Bonita complex with her neighbor (Johanna Stein). She moves from apartment #12 to #17 to hide from Ed's backers, who are looking for her. Meanwhile, Camilla tries to reconnect with Diane and even sleeps with her again. However, one day, after a little romp on Diane's couch, Camilla ends the relationship for good. Offended, Diane rejects any further advances from her love. Nevertheless, she hopes that Camilla will leave Adam and return to her. She does not want to accept the final separation.

But Camilla finally makes up her mind: she stays with Adam. During a film rehearsal in which Camilla plays the leading role and Diane plays a supporting role arranged by her, Camilla makes it clear to Diane once again that she no longer wants a relationship. She kisses Adam provocatively in front of Diane.

When Camilla calls Diane some time later to invite her to a surprise, Diane has new hope. But the surprise turns out to be an invitation to Camilla and Adam's engagement party - another humiliation. At the party, Camilla kisses another woman (Melissa George) in front of Diane and then announces her planned marriage to Adam. At the next table, Diane discovers her suitor Luigi looking at her lustfully. Diane's panic reaches its peak: she feels exploited, humiliated and betrayed by everyone around her.

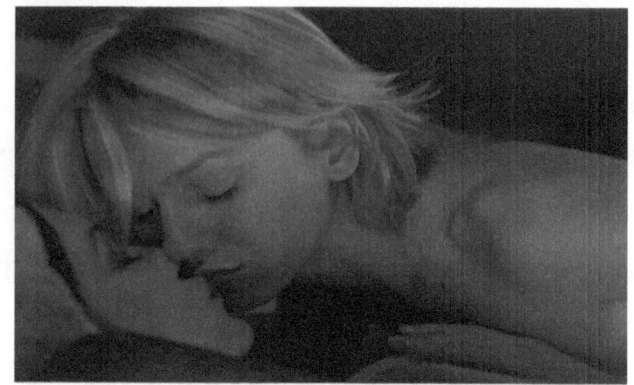

Camilla kisses Diane

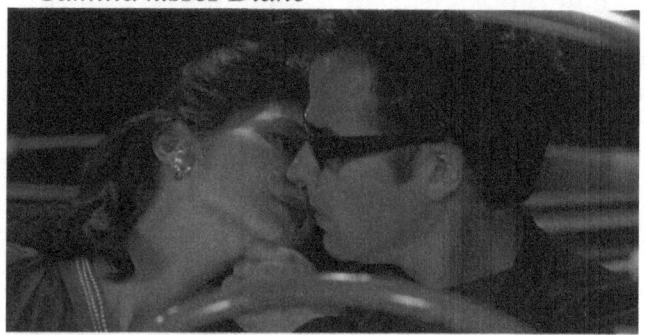

Camilla kisses Adam

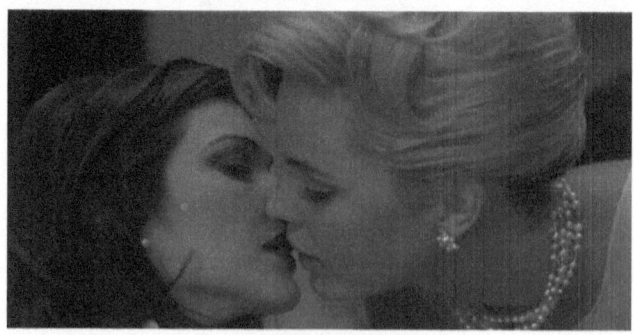

Camilla kisses another woman

At this point, Diane finally loses her mind. She decides to put an end to it and hires Joe to kill Camilla. However, the hitman demands a considerable sum for this murder, as he sees no personal gain in it. In desperation, Diane sleeps with Mr. Roque to obtain the necessary money. Her hatred of Camilla eclipses her disgust for him.

At Winkie's, Diane hands Joe the required sum and a photo of Camilla. The killer shows her a blue key that she is to find behind the restaurant as soon as the murder has been carried out. Diane dares to go to the agreed-upon location behind the restaurant, fearing the worst, and discovers the key. Camilla is dead - there is no turning back. Diane flees to her apartment with the key and falls into a deep, long sleep. When her neighbor wakes her with a loud knock, she realizes that she is a murderer: the blue key is lying on her table. She begins to hallucinate. In her delusion, Camilla suddenly appears alive and at home. Diane makes coffee to wake her up and clear her head.

But the bad memories catch up with her. In her mind's eye, she revisits the past few days: the break-up, the humiliation during the shoot, the engagement party, and finally the meeting with the killer at Winkie's.

There is a knock at the door. Diane knows that it is the detectives (Robert Forster, Brent Briscoe) who are looking for her as a murder suspect. She hallucinates that her grandparents are crawling out from under the doorstep. Driven by mortal fear, she flees to her bedroom, grabs a pistol from the bedside drawer, and shoots herself. At the moment of her death, she once again sees Camilla and herself in a happy moment. Then the monster from her dream appears in the place where she found the key. Finally, she considers an actress from Club Silencio (Cori Glazer), who speaks the last word: "Silencio!" The movie and Diane's life come to an end.

The life of Diane Selwyn: from happiness to sadness to despair

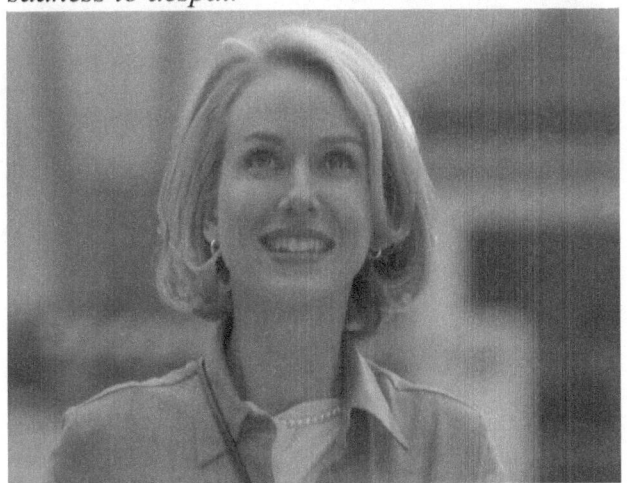

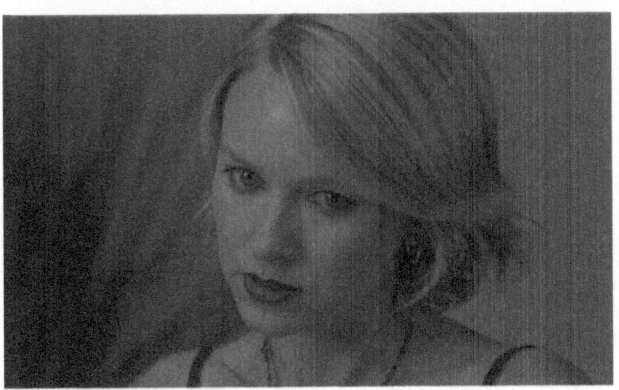

42

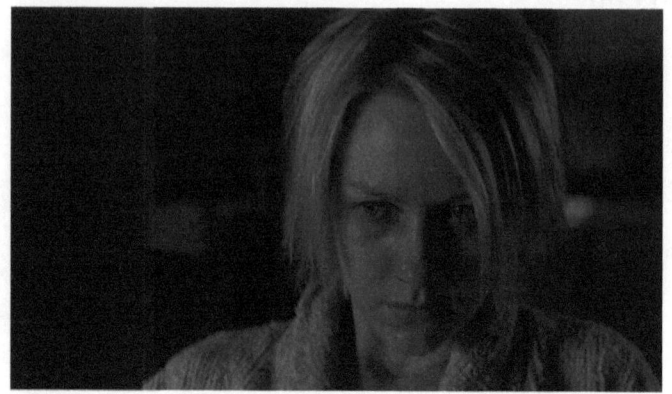

PLAY OF A DREAMER: A STEP-BY-STEP ANALYSIS OF MULHOLLAND DRIVE

Once the chronology of *Mulholland Drive* has been assigned to the various narrative levels and we have reconstructed Diane's life using clues from her dream and her memories shortly before her death, we can begin with the interpretations. To do this, we need to analyze and decipher Diane's dream in detail.

It should be noted that it is not possible to explain a dream linearly. Dreams are usually a jumbled sequence of scenes. Yet, they can be interpreted if you realize that they symbolically and metaphorically reflect the reality and emotions of the dreamer through images. What has happened, as well as all fears, longings, and desires, are processed, changed, and continued in the dream.

Diane's dream provides fundamental information that can be used to substantiate the theory of Diane's actual life story presented in the previous chapter. In the following analysis, all significant dream characters, locations, and symbols are examined in the context of Diane's life in reality and her memories of the past.

Within this step-by-step analysis, all of Lynch's indications for interpreting *Mulholland Drive* are also taken into account. However, the presentation does not follow Lynch's predetermined order. If a chapter explicitly refers to one of the clues, this is marked accordingly.

A contract killing in a restaurant

In her final nightmare, Diane comes to terms with terrible events: sexual abuse by her father, her failed Hollywood career, her job as a prostitute, and her jealousy of Camilla's death, for which she is responsible. From Diane's memories of the past, depicted later in the movie, we know that she ordered Joe to murder her at a table in Winkie's restaurant. She hands him a photo of Camilla and the money he demands. Since we are in the Mulholland Drive decryption, we naturally start with the key at this point.

Lynch's clue no. 5: Who gives whom a key - and why?

Joe shows Diane a blue key and tells her that she will find the key at a prearranged location "when it's done". This place is undoubtedly the ledge behind Winkie's. This is shown in the following scene. Behind it sits a homeless man—or "the monster" (Bonnie Aarons)—who is playing with a blue box to which the key belongs. "The monster" wraps the box in a bag, out of which we see the elderly couple, Diane's grandparents, walking, who are shown at the airport at the beginning of the movie. They laugh sinisterly.

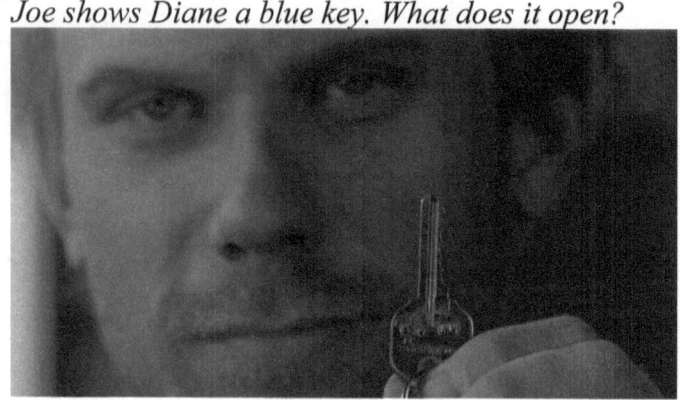

Joe shows Diane a blue key. What does it open?

FROM THE DANCE INTO THE WILD DREAM

Lynch's clue no. 1: Pay special attention to the beginning of the movie. Two important clues can be found even before the opening title.

We are in the opening scene of the movie *Mulholland Drive*, experiencing one of Diane's happiest moments in life: a cinematic collage of couples dancing at a jitterbug dance contest, which Diane wins. She is shown overjoyed in a winning pose together with her grinning grandparents, whom she has probably made proud for the first time. At this moment, her grandparents accept her ambition to become an actress and support her wish to move to Hollywood after the death of her Aunt Ruth.

In the next scene of the movie, we see the blue key lying on Diane's living room table. We are now in the present reality. Diane has found the key at the agreed location and taken it home with her. Now she knows for sure that Camilla is dead and that she is a contract killer. In Diane's dream, Rita also finds a blue key in her pocket. However, it is shaped differently, which indicates that we are in the dream level. So there are two blue keys: one that marks reality and one that suggests the dream plane.

In a very short scene that follows, we see a

bed with pink pillows and a green comforter. Someone is breathing deeply in and out. We do not know this person, but it is Diane who falls into her pillow from the first-person perspective and falls asleep. This happens after she has found the blue key and taken it home with her. Diane wants to "sleep away" her problems. This scene also takes place in the present reality. From this moment on, a long, wild dream begins.

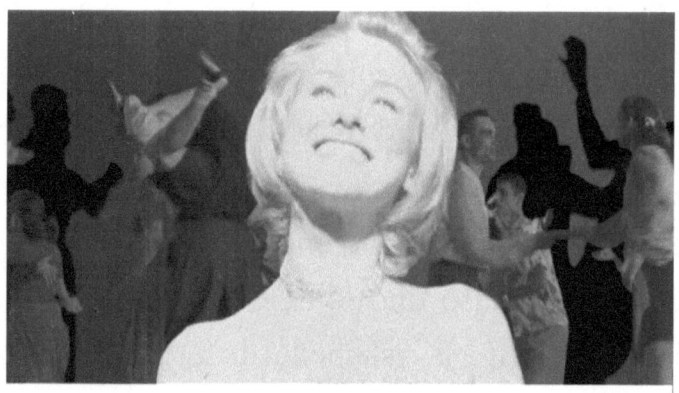

Diane wins the Jitterbug dance competition

A MONSTER BEHIND WINKIE'S

Lynch's clue no. 9: Keep a close eye on what's going on around the man behind Winkie's.

During her conversation about the contract killing with Joe, Diane notices a man (Patrick Fischler) in Winkie's who looks at her fearfully. In her dream, she gives him the name "Dan". The similarity between her name, "Diane," and his shows a close connection between them and his feelings. Dan is a part of herself in the dream. In reality, Diane feels caught out by Dan's gaze, as if he has a premonition or might have seen through her plan.

In Diane's dream, Dan is sitting in Winkie's with his psychiatrist, Herb (Michael Cooke), and tells him of his great fear of this place and of something horrible that is about to happen. In reality, Herb is probably Diane's therapist, but he was unable to help her. Diane had turned to a behavioral therapist who offers confrontation therapy, as seen in the example of Dan. However, she would have needed a therapist who could work with her psychoanalytically on her childhood traumas. However, she probably shied away from analyzing her past.

Dan mentions that he had previously dreamt of this very meeting with his psychiatrist in the same setting and feels like he is in a dream. He is in one - but not his own, but Diane's. It is a dream within a dream. Dan becomes even more frightened when Herb goes to the spot in front of the cash register where Dan saw him in his dream and looks over at him. In Diane's real past, "Dan" is standing in this exact spot when she notices him talking to Joe.

In the dream, Dan accompanies his psychiatrist to the ledge of the wall that he had dreamed about, behind which he expects evil. This is exactly where Diane found the blue key in reality. Through Dan, Diane experiences the same thing again in her dream that she did when she approached the wall: the moment she found the key, she was scared to death. This fear is translated in her dream by "the monster", who scares Dan to death.

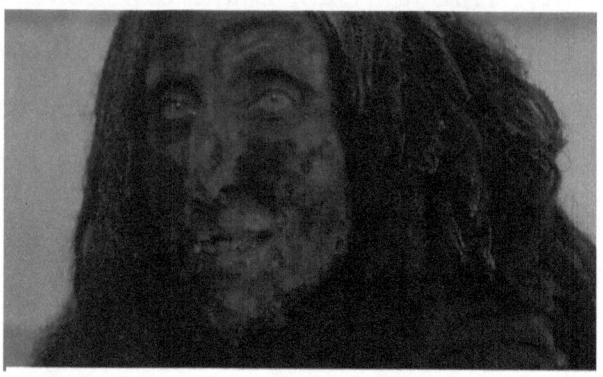
A monster lurks behind Winkie's

THE BIRTH OF BETTY ELMS - AND HOW CAMILLA BECOMES RITA

On the one hand, Diane's subconscious gets rid of a potential accomplice to the contract killing through Dan's death, because he observed her talking to Joe. Secondly, she can free herself from her guilty conscience: she doesn't want to admit Camilla's death and would have preferred to die in Dan's place.

In her dreams, Diane wishes that everything had turned out differently than in reality - that she could start again, become successful herself, and get to know Camilla again.

So she creates the fictional Betty, whose name she chooses as she sits with Joe in Winkie's and reads the nameplate of the waitress of the same name. In the dream, Betty becomes exactly the person Diane always wanted to be: charismatic, talented, popular, and successful. She creates a model image of herself that psychoanalyst Sigmund Freud describes as an "idealized self". Her new surname becomes "Elms". Perhaps Diane once saw the movie *Nightmare on Elm Street*, in which she is warned against what she is doing: dreaming!

Lynch's clue #4: An accident is a terrible event. Pay close attention to the location of the accident.

The black sedan accident occurs in Diane's dream near Adam's mansion at 6980 Mulholland

Drive. Diane dreams of two men driving Camilla along Mulholland Drive. They stop in the middle of the road, threaten her with a gun, and try to force her to get out of the car - presumably to kill her.

The place is the same one where Diane was chauffeured in the past and from which Camilla picked her up for the pool party afterwards. Diane has also been forced to get out of the car, figuratively speaking. This is the last time she has any hope that Camilla will return to her; after all, Camilla has promised her a surprise. But the surprise was not the one she had hoped for: At the party, Camilla announces her marriage to Adam, humiliating Diane. The sentence that the dream Camilla says to her kidnappers ("What are you doing? We're not stopping here.") was told by Diane herself to her chauffeur (Scott Wulff) when she wondered why he was stopping in the middle of the road.

Before the dream, Camilla can get out of the

car; however, an accident occurs. A car crashes into the limousine without braking. The dream Camilla is not killed, survives the accident, loses her memory, and later becomes Rita (Laura Elena Harring) after hiding in Aunt Ruth's apartment. This allows Betty to begin a whole new love affair with this strange woman, without Camilla/Rita knowing who she is. Diane's subconscious has prevented Camilla's death in the alternative history of the accident. Rita's amnesia makes it possible for the "better Diane" - Betty - to fall in love with Camilla/Rita effortlessly.

The money that Rita brings to Betty in her bag would certainly have been useful to Diane at this point in reality. She would have been broke by the time she hired Joe as a hitman. There is also considerably more money in her pocket than Diane had to pay for the murder. The desperate search for sources of money plays a central role in Diane's life. However, she makes provisions for her dream, Betty.

After Rita thinks she remembers having an accident on Mulholland Drive, Betty suggests calling the police. She wants to find out if such an accident happened there the previous night. Rita feels uneasy at the thought, but Betty reassures her by saying they could do it like in the movies - and pretend to be someone else. That's probably what Diane loved so much about acting: being able to be someone else. And that's exactly what she does with Betty as her alter ego. In her dream, she can slip perfectly into another role.

At Winkie's restaurant, Diane and Rita later sit in the same place where Diane sat during the job interview with Joe. There, Diane notices the waitress's (Melissa Crider) name tag, which reads "Diane". In reality, Diane sees the name "Betty" on the same waitress's name tag, which later inspires her to name the dream character after it.

In the dream, this waitress, who looks very much like Diane herself, then becomes "Betty" because Diane once worked here. When Rita becomes aware of the waitress, she can remember "Diane Selwyn" - in other words, "Betty's" real name. The dreaming Diane gets a little closer to her Camilla again: Rita has forgotten almost everything, but not Betty's real name as "Camilla"! So that's how important it must be to Camilla/Rita - at least that's how Diane's dream interprets it.

Rita and Betty look for "D. Selwyn" in the phone book and call the number. As they dial the number, Betty confesses to Rita that it is strange to call herself. This is another hidden clue, because she calls herself in the dream. Rita replies: "Maybe it's not me." A sentence that is apt in two respects: firstly, she is not Diane Selwyn and secondly, she is not even Rita.

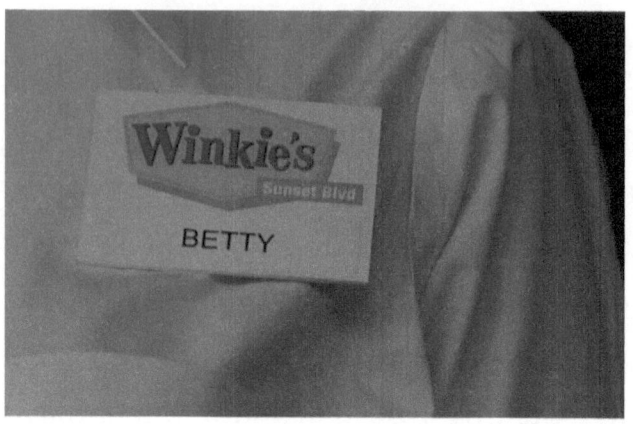

Betty serves at Winkie's

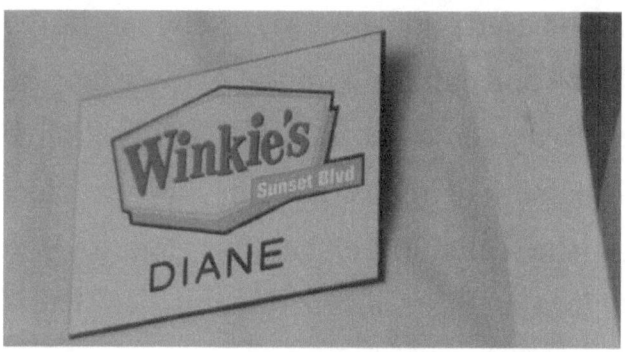

Diane also serves at Winkie's

A BOTCHED CASTING AND A SAD DIRECTOR

Lynch's clue #3: Pay attention to what the title of the movie, Adam Kesher, is auditioning and watching actresses for. Is this title repeated elsewhere?

Diane dreams about her actual audition for the *Sylvia North story*. Betty walks through the gate to the production site, full of pride and anticipation. The scene almost seems like a remake of the scene in which she walks through the gate to the Havenhurst apartment complex at the beginning of the movie. Her acting partner for the chosen scene, Woody Katz (Chad Everett), reveals that he has previously rehearsed with a black-haired woman—a clear reference to Camilla, who ultimately gets the role in reality.

After the audition, everyone present in the dream is thrilled by Betty's talent, which she impressively demonstrates. Her acting is extremely spontaneous and highly emotional. However, Diane probably didn't come across as convincing in reality as Betty did in her dream. The director Bob does not want to cast her in the role in reality. In the dream, however, he is portrayed as incompetent and ignorant: He almost falls asleep, is off his game, and is laughed at by those present. Diane's subconscious blames Bob's supposed incompetence for the fact that she was ultimately not considered for the role.

After the audition, the invited star cast member, Linny James (Rita Taggart), who could hardly have been hired for a low-budget production like this, and her assistant, Nicki Pelazza (Michele Hicks), get upset with producer Wally. Linny says, "Oh God, that was awful." Nicki adds, "Woody is only doing the casting as a favor to Wally." In the dream, these statements refer to Wally's incompetence, but in reality, they probably refer to Diane's disappointing performance. Betty registers these remarks in the dream with a skeptical, almost shocked look.

In another scene, Diane dreams that Adam is directing the *Sylvia North story*. Linny announces him as an outstanding director who is working on a project that Betty "would kill for," according to Linny. A fateful sentence, because Diane has killed for this project.

Adam is casting female singers in a big studio. Betty gets to listen to the song *Sixteen Reasons* by Connie Stevens:

"... Sixteen reasons why I love you
One: the way you hold my hand
Two: your laughing eyes
Three: the way you understand
Four: your secret sighs
They're all part of sixteen reasons why I love you ..."

A song that Diane probably enjoyed listening to when she was happy with Camilla. The number 16 plays a recurring role throughout the movie *Mulholland Drive*, especially in Diane's living conditions. She lives with her aunt at 1612 Havenhurst and later in room number 16 at the Park Hotel. Even the Sierra Bonita apartment complex, where she moves in with Camilla, has the address 2590 - the sum of the digits also adds up to 16. This number seems to play a decisive role in Diane's life. It is possible that her parents died when she was 16, and she has had to live with her grandparents ever since.

Another song that Diane hears at the *Sylvia North Story* audition is Linda Scott's *I've Told Every Little Star*:

"... Maybe, you may love me too. Oh, my darling, if you do. Why haven't you told me ..."

A song that Diane must have enjoyed

listening to when she still had hope that Camilla would return to her after the separation.

Adam's casting for the *Sylvia North story* never took place in reality. In the dream, however, the director looks at Betty with great infatuation, almost as if he is in love, as if he desperately wants to cast her in his movie. However, he can't, because Luigi and Vincenzo Castigliane (Dan Hedaya) have ordered him to give Camilla Rhodes the role; otherwise, he would lose his job. However, the Camilla Rhodes in Diane's dream is a different person from the real Camilla. In the photo shown at Adam's meeting with the Castigliane brothers and later on the show stage, the blonde woman, Diane, can be seen kissing "her" Camilla at Adam's pool party in her past, as seen in real life.

At this point in the dream, Diane's subconscious suggests to her that a big conspiracy has prevented her from getting the part in the *Sylvia North story*. At the same time, she enjoys the idea that Adam, who gets together with Camilla, would have desired her.

From Diane's memories of the past, we learn that she met Camilla during rehearsals for the Sylvia North story at the pool party. Diane tells us, visibly sad, that Camilla got the part—a role that Diane herself would have loved to have had and which might have made her famous.

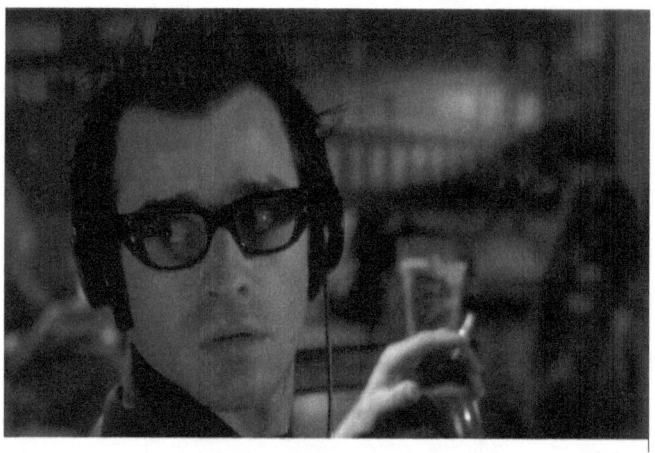

Adam catches sight of Betty. He is not allowed to cast her in the lead role.

REVERSED ROLES: A DREAM POOL PARTY

Lynch's clue no. 10: Where is "Aunt Ruth"?

Adam's pool party is one of the pivotal scenes in deciphering *Mulholland Drive*. It took place, and Diane remembers it after she wakes up. Important basic information about Diane's story is revealed in this section. She tells Coco (Ann Miller), Adam's mother, that she is from Deep River, Ontario - information that Betty shared with Rita earlier in the movie during the dream. Diane's formulation that she has just been there and is now "in this dream city" is remarkable— a linguistic allusion by the director to the dreaming Diane and her illusion of "Hollywood."

At the pool party, Diane also talks about the jitterbug dance competition she won, which led her to Hollywood. She also talks about her recently deceased Aunt Ruth, who worked in the movie business and left her some money. In Diane's dream, however, Ruth is at film rehearsals in Canada. Diane never got the chance to see Ruth before she died. To make this loss more bearable, she imagines in her dream that Ruth is only temporarily abroad.

There is a saying in the US film business: "If you have to shoot in Canada, you're already dead." So it's no coincidence that Diane imagines the neighboring country with its manageable film industry as Ruth's place of residence. The original English version speaks of "Aunt Ruth". Lynch's affinity for ambiguous naming in his films suggests that "Aunt Ruth" can also be interpreted as "Untruth": it's not true; she's not in Canada; she's dead.

The dream character Louise Bonner (Lee Grant), who warns Betty at the door of Aunt Ruth's apartment that something bad is about to happen, also claims that Ruth is not Betty's aunt. She's right, because Ruth is Diane's aunt, not Betty's.

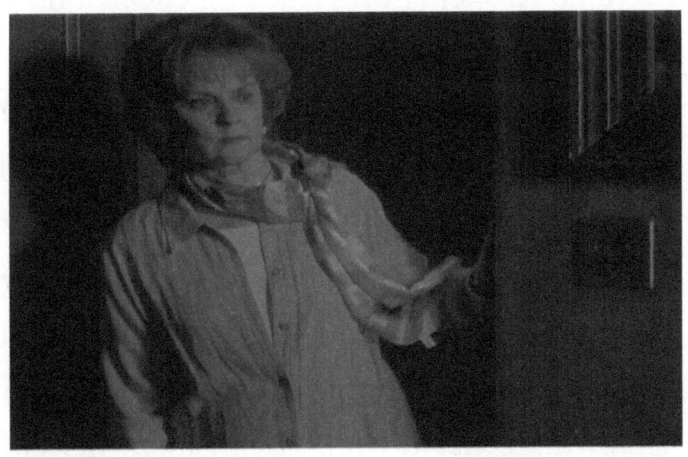

Aunt Ruth - Untruth?

At the pool party, Diane also tells us how she met Camilla during rehearsals for the *Sylvia North story*. Camilla got the part that Diane was "so keen" on, but the director, Bob, didn't think much of her. She reports that she then became friends with Camilla and got a few smaller roles in films as a result.

At the party, Diane notices Adam flirting heavily with Camilla. He tells a short story from which Diane can gather that his ex-wife, Lorraine Kesher (Lori Heuring), cheated on him with a pool cleaner.

Diane vividly embellishes this story in her dream: She dreams of Adam catching Lorraine in flagrante delicto in bed with pool cleaner Gene (Billy Ray Cyrus). She wishes Adam, who has taken her love from her, all the worst and wants him to go through a similar horror trip to her own. In her dream, Adam loses his entire fortune, which was presumably the incentive for Camilla to enter into a relationship with him in the first place. In the end, Adam has to stay in Cookie's Park Hotel, where Diane once had to live herself. But in her dream, the situation is reversed: Cookie demands money from Adam, not from Diane - so she swaps roles with the director.

Adam's secretary, Cynthia Jenzen (Katharine

Towne), tries to seduce him and offers him a place to sleep. Adam, however, shows no interest. There is also a specific intention behind this: Diane wishes Adam had also rejected Camilla when she tried to seduce him. Lorraine finally kicks her husband out of his own house after he catches her with Gene. Adam loses his job, money, and wife, satisfaction for Diane.

Her desire for revenge is also evident in the scene in which Adam's clothes are completely stained with pink paint after he has smeared his wife's jewelry with the same color. Pink is the color of Diane and Betty - more on that later.

Even though Diane mixes up stories about and around Adam in her dream, he remains a dream figure modeled on the real Adam. It is similar to Joe, the contract killer, with whom the dreamer also settles accounts. In her dream, Joe is depicted as an extremely clumsy killer who shoots two innocent people. This could reflect Diane's wishful thinking that, in reality, Joe might not have killed Camilla after all, or might have gotten the wrong person. Subconsciously, Diane wants nothing more than for Camilla to be alive.

However, in Diane's dream, Joe kills her pimp Ed in cold blood. This murder could have occurred. This has come as a great relief to Diane, as Ed has been pressuring her to sleep with Johns she has been disgusted by.

Joe steals Ed's "famous black book" from his office, which contains the names of his call girls and clients. Diane has probably told Joe about this book in real life, which Ed describes as "the history of our world in phone numbers" - a clue to its significance. Joe stole this book; it's on the table at Winkie's during the job interview between Diane and him. Joe probably killed Ed in real life to eliminate a competitor and blackmail the names in the book.

In the scene in Winkie's where Joe is sitting at the table with Diane, he has deep blue eyes.

This eye color is accentuated by the blue key he holds in front of him. In the sequence in which Joe is in Ed's office, however, he has one brown and one blue eye - another dream translation. Blue stands for the bitter truth: Camilla will be dead. But the fact that Joe only has one blue eye in the dream shows Diane's inner conflict. On the one hand, she wishes for Camilla's death, but on the other, she hopes that her lover is still alive and that she will escape with a black eye.

Some other roles are reversed in Diane's dream. Real people are assigned different roles. One example is Adam's mother, Coco, who becomes the scatterbrained but lovable landlady Coco Lenoix (Ann Miller) in Diane's dream. At the pool party, Coco says to Diane: "Oh, call me Coco, that's what everyone does." Diane has memorized this sentence well, because in her dream, Coco says the same thing to Betty when she introduces herself. She is also wearing the same black and red dress.

Coco seems to be the only one at the pool party who is interested in Diane. In her dream, she helps Betty: she hands her the script for the audition, wishes her luck, and turns a blind eye when Rita spends the night with her. Coco eats walnuts from a bowl at the pool party. So the dream surname Lenoix (French: *les noix*: walnuts) suits her. Diane brings a touch of humor to her dream with this name (Coco Lenoix, French: noix de coco, meaning "coconut").

The cowboy (Lafayette Montgomery), who plays a special fateful role in Diane's dream and "convinces" Adam to hire Camilla instead of Diane, is also a guest at the party. In the dream, he threatens Adam: "You'll see me again if you do it right. You'll see me twice more if you do it wrong." Adam allows himself to be intimidated, gets it "right" by casting blonde Camilla and, in Diane's dream logic, sees the cowboy once again in reality - at his party.

According to Diane's dream logic, the party she remembers takes place after the cowboy meets with Adam, as Camilla is already engaged at this point. Diane herself sees the cowboy twice: when he wakes her up and at the party. She knows she has done "it" wrong.

At the pool party, Diane notices a blonde girl kissing Camilla to humiliate her. This girl builds Diane into her dream as Camilla Rhodes—a second Camilla, embodied by another woman.

Luigi, a suitor with whom Diane reluctantly had to sleep, sits at the next table at the party and looks at her lustfully while she drinks a coffee. No wonder he is depicted as repulsive in her dream: There, Luigi spits out his espresso and looks dissatisfied. Diane feels disgusted by coffee at this moment. Lynch intensifies the menace of this scene by having Diane drink from a cup with "SOS" written on it.

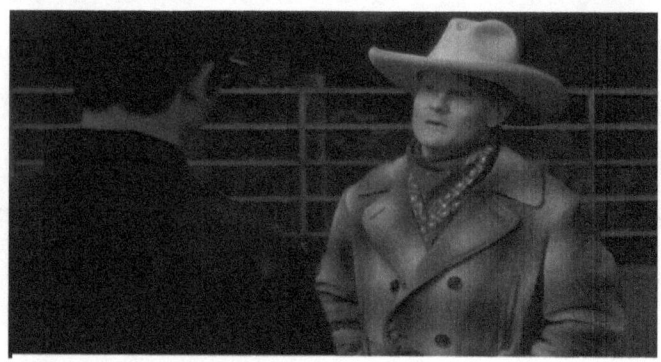
The cowboy blackmails Adam

Camilla's way into the limelight

Lynch's clue no. 8: Does Camilla's talent alone help her?

Camilla undoubtedly seems to have talent, but she can't rely on that alone. To secure more and, above all, larger roles, she approaches Adam, leaves Diane, and moves out of the apartment they share in apartment 12 of the Sierra Bonita complex. The relationship between Betty and Rita, which seems familiar from the outset, suggests that Diane and Camilla lived together. One clue to this is Diane's line when she goes to the audition in her dream: "Don't drink all the Coke!" When Betty calls Diane Selwyn's house and Rita doesn't recognize the voice, she gives us another clue: "Maybe you have a roommate."

Camilla has probably not been an official prostitute, but has slept with influential men in return for support in the film industry. At the pool party, she proudly says: "Yo nunca fuí a Casablanca con Luigi" ("I never went to Casablanca with Luigi"). By this, she means that she was never intimate with Luigi, knowing full well that Diane was. The movie *Casablanca* is about refugees who can exchange visas - and therefore freedom - for sex with the police chief. Camilla may be referring to this movie. However, it is more likely that "Casablanca" is the name of a hotel or restaurant where Luigi met with prostitutes. Both actually exist in Los

Angeles. Coco looks skeptical at this moment, as she knows that Camilla has come up with an unconventional way to get the ball rolling.

Camilla seems to have a very permissive sexuality anyway. When she kisses the "wrong" blonde Camilla at the pool party, her fiancé Adam is not at all bothered. What the "fake" Camilla whispers to the real one before the kiss is only audible as a mumble in the German dubbed version. Even in the original English version, the utterance can only be heard very quietly, but it can be read from the lips of the 'fake' Camilla: "I am going to take a walk outside. Give me a kiss!" The kiss between the two women seems very intimate and familiar. Afterwards, the "fake" Camilla looks at Diane, and the imprint of Camilla's lipstick is etched on her lips. Diane begins to cry. It is conceivable that the "fake" Camilla is also already a respected actress with whom Camilla has had a romantic relationship to expand her connections.

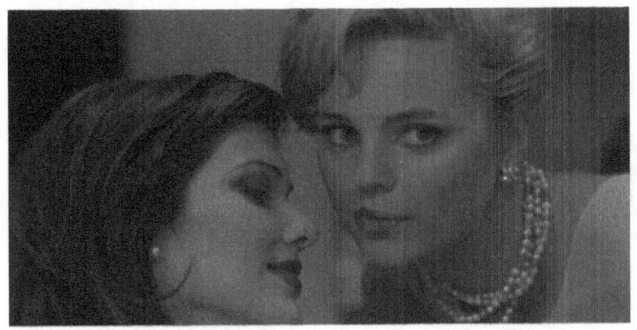
Two Camillas, double humiliation for Diane

HIDDEN CLUES: DIANE'S CHILD ABUSE AND HER RED LIGHT ACTIVITY

There are numerous indications that Diane was sexually abused in her childhood. However, Lynch does not let the viewer know directly at any point that this was the case. Some symbolic clues can be found in Aunt Ruth's apartment, where the painting "Beatrice Cenci" by the painter Guido Reni hangs. Beatrice Cenci was a 16th-century Roman patrician who was abused by her extremely brutal father, Francesco Cenci, and eventually had him killed. She was executed for this at the age of 22.

On a shelf diagonally in front of the painting is a black and white photo of a woman with a little blonde girl in her arms - presumably Aunt Ruth with Diane. This could represent a possible dream connection to Diane's sexual abuse at a young age.

Rita Hayworth, whose poster hangs in Aunt Ruth's bathroom and whose first name the nameless Camilla chooses, is also said to have been sexually abused by her father, Eduardo Cansino. There are several parallels to Hayworth: She suffered from Alzheimer's in the last phase of her life, while Rita Hayworth suffered from amnesia. A studio boss forced Rita Hayworth to change her father's name to Cansino because he didn't like it. She had to take her mother's name, "Hayworth" - similar to Camilla, who had also changed her name.

The movie *Sylvia North Story* is fictional, but in 1965, a film entitled *The Past Life of Sylvia West* (original: *Sylvia*) was released. In it, Sylvia West is abused by her stepfather and later becomes a prostitute. During the casting for the *Sylvia North story* in Diane's Dream, her partner Woody makes ambiguous remarks. He begins with the sentence: "Just say where it hurts, baby." A sentence that could also be uttered in a typical, arranged doctor game. Betty responds and plays the role extremely freely. At this moment, she feels compelled to "satisfy" the filmmakers present just as she once did her father. Diane is probably so "keen" on the role because she can put herself in the shoes of Sylvia West - or Sylvia North.

Diane comes from Deep River in Ontario. Deep River is also the name of the apartment in Lynch's film *Blue Velvet*, in which Frank rapes Dorothy. Lynch is once again playing with names. Betty doesn't mention her parents once in the entire movie, which is very unusual. It seems as if she has suppressed her parents: her father, because he abused her, and her mother, because she watched and did nothing. Only the car accident, in which her parents presumably died, has burned itself into her subconscious and is processed as a drastic experience in her dreams.

Lynch's clue no. 2: Note the appearance of the red lampshade

In *Mulholland Drive*, the red lampshades tell us when we are in Diane's apartment. Diane dreams about how Mr. Roque usually tries to contact her: through a telephone chain via an intermediary, and Ed. When her phone rings in the dream, it may also ring in reality, and she incorporates this into her dream. We see the red lampshade next to a full ashtray and the phone. We later learn from Diane's memories that this is her bedside table. She makes a call on this very phone next to the red lampshade and speaks to Camilla, who invites her to a surprise.

Mr. Roque is an important figure in Diane's dream. She is disgusted by him and refuses him her services after a single meeting. However, Mr. Roque refuses to accept this. He says on the phone, "The girl is still missing." Later, Diane gets over herself and sleeps with him to get the money for the contract killing. The sleeping Diane does not pick up the phone when Mr. Roque tries to contact her.

In Diane's dream, Mr. Roque becomes the central figure behind the casting instructions for Adam and the boss of the Castigliane brothers. He orders an intermediary to cancel the production. This reinterpretation of reality reflects Diane's hope that Camilla will not be able to play the role in the *Sylvia North story*.

The red lampshades can also symbolize Diane's activities in the red light district. She probably met her clients behind Pink's restaurant. In the dream, Joe talks to the prostitute Laney (Rena Riffel). Next to Pink's is an antique store, in the window of which a red lampshade can also be seen.

Further references to Diane's street prostitution activities can be found in this scene. Laney looks quite similar to Diane and even wears the same brand of jeans. A man with an overlong red stick walks past Joe and Laney as if to separate the street from the red light district. The hot dog on the previously shown Pink's advertising sign symbolizes a phallus. The garbage can in the side street is also red. A blue van, which Laney gets into, is parked directly in front of a men's restroom.

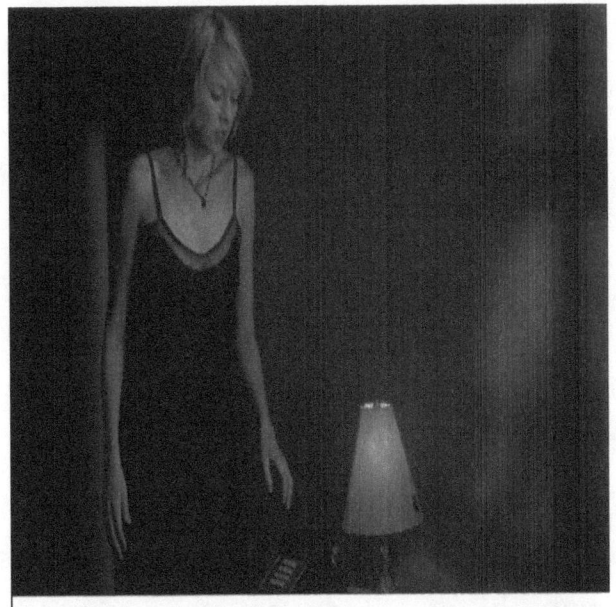

Diane's phone is next to a lamp with a red shade

COLOR AND NUMBER GAMES

Lynch's clue no. 6: Pay close attention to the clothes, the ashtray, the cup of coffee.

The clothing of the main characters plays a central role in *Mulholland Drive*, especially in terms of color. Rita mainly wears black or red. Black symbolizes mourning - Diane mourns the death of Camilla and is therefore often seen wearing black. Red, on the other hand, represents love, passion, and power, which aligns with the real-life Camilla, who predominantly wears red clothing. The name "Rhodes" (ancient Greek: Rhodes, English: rose) was probably chosen deliberately by Lynch.

Rita wears two different black and red bathrobes: a black one with red roses at the beginning of the film, which Aunt Ruth has left in her apartment for Betty, and a red bathrobe with a black collar in the rehearsal scene for the audition.

The dream, Betty, on the other hand, often wears pink or baby blue. Pink represents childlike naivety, fragility, and self-contempt - characteristics that suit Diane and, by extension, Betty. Pink could also be linked to Betty's work as a prostitute, as Diane had her regular spot behind Pink's restaurant. In the scene in which Betty and Rita practice Diane's audition, Diane wears a pink bathrobe and behaves childishly. Rita, on the other hand, wears a red bathrobe and appears serious and professional. She is puzzled by Betty's childish optimism, but compliments her as a professional: "You're really good."

In the present reality, Diane sleeps in pink sheets but wears a white bathrobe. The white bathrobe is a sign that we are now in reality and no longer in a dream.

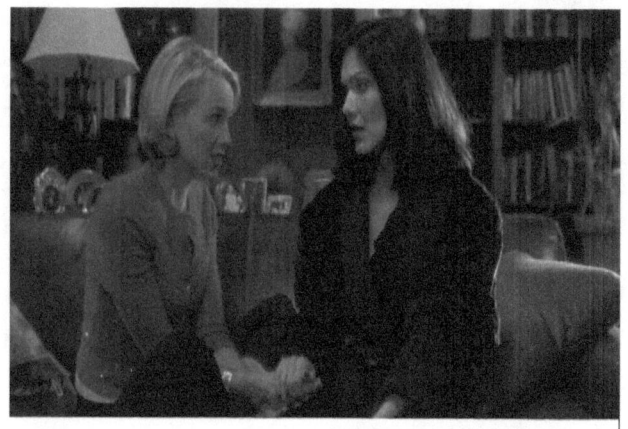

*Betty likes to wear pink, Rita black and red.
The Beatrice Cenci painting in the background*

When Rita and Betty set off to visit Diane Selwyn, they see on the residents' sign in the Sierra Bonita apartment complex that Diane lives in apartment number 12. But when they knock on the door, a dark-haired woman answers and tells them that she and Diane have swapped apartments. She now lives in number 12, while Diane can be found in number 17.

At this point, David Lynch gives us one of the biggest mysteries of the movie: Did Diane swap apartments with the woman, and if so, why? And who is this dark-haired woman anyway? The name "L. J. DeRosa" is written next to apartment number 12 on the resident's sign in the apartment complex, so we refer to her as DeRosa and assume that the apartment swap took place. The moving boxes in Diane's apartment speak for themselves.

It is also DeRosa who wakes Diane from her confused dream by knocking on her apartment door. When Diane opens, DeRosa asks for her lamp and dishes, both of which she has left at Diane's place. She also notices a piano ashtray, which also belongs to her and is on the table next to the blue key. This is an indication that we are in the present reality.

The two women seem familiar, yet at odds with each other at the same time. It's possible that they had a love affair and broke up, but there is insufficient evidence to support that. For some reason, however, Diane has asked DeRosa to swap apartments with her. It is possible that Diane no longer feels comfortable or safe after Camilla moved out of apartment 12. DeRosa mentions that the swap was three weeks ago.

The timeline of *Mulholland Drive* remains unclear at this point. When did Camilla's murder happen? It is unlikely that it happened three weeks ago and that Diane wanted to swap apartments to avoid being found. It is equally doubtful that she swapped apartments because it reminded her of Camilla - after all, we later learn that Camilla is still lying naked on the couch with Diane in apartment number 17.

However, Diane is already severely depressed at the time of the swap, as indicated by the unpacked boxes. The swap could have happened because Diane wanted to hide from someone. DeRosa seems annoyed in reality and the dream, presumably because she has been asked about Diane several times before. Significantly, her phone rings when Betty and

Rita ask about Diane in the dream. It is possible that DeRosa denied Diane after she asked her to do so, perhaps even in exchange for Diane's money.

One reason for Diane's hiding could have been trouble on the streets, possibly in connection with Ed's murder. Although Ed no longer has his "black book", Diane could have been associated with him. Mr. Roque or his middleman may have been looking for her. The detectives may also have already been looking for her, because of Ed's murder.

Camilla's murder was probably no more than a day or two ago at this point. DeRosa mentions that the detectives had asked about Diane for the second time, presumably in connection with Camilla's murder. Joe could have been caught, and Diane's name could have been in the "black book". Since it was known to many that Diane and Camilla were friends, the detectives would have questioned DeRosa a second time.

Shortly after DeRosa leaves the apartment in the present reality, there is another knock on Diane's door. It's the detectives. Diane suspects this, flees to her bedroom, and shoots herself. *Silencio!* But there is still no peace - there are more clues.

Diane is a non-smoker; at least we don't see her smoke once in the movie. Camilla, on the other hand, smokes and often wears conspicuous red lipstick. On Diane's bedside table next to the red lampshade is a full ashtray with a red cigarette butt. It is possible that Diane does not empty the ashtray of Camilla's cigarettes, which she probably smoked after sex, to keep a familiar part of her with her.

The brown ceramic coffee cups in Diane's apartment are identical to those at Winkie'*s*. This could be an indication that Diane worked there and took the cups with her. Diane often drinks coffee in real life. In one scene, a camera pan shows how the coffee cup suddenly becomes a

Coke when Diane remembers the past and joins the naked Camilla on the sofa. In this flashback, Diane is no longer wearing jeans, but her bathrobe - a cinematically successful transition between present reality and the remembered past.

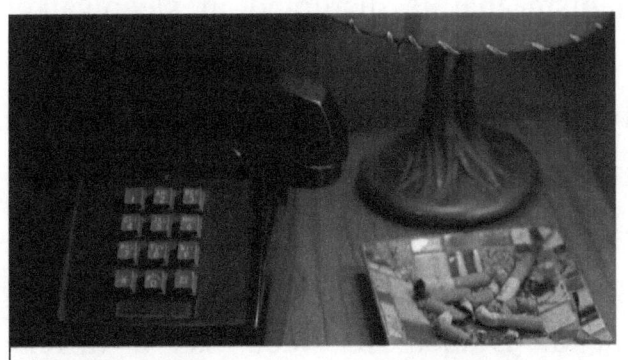

Diane's bedside cabinet is full of clues.

The corpse (Lyssie Powell) that Betty and Rita find in Diane's apartment in Sierra Bonita is in the same position that Diane is in before she wakes up. Diane is dreaming of her death at this moment. This makes it clear that Diane has already decided to kill herself before or during her dream.

Some people, like Diane in her last dream phase, experience lucid dreams in which they see themselves from above. In these lucid moments, often accompanied by natural sleep paralysis, the body appears to be paralyzed—a protective mechanism that is disrupted in sleepwalkers. Diane may have experienced such sleep paralysis, seeing herself from above and thus imagining her death in the same position.

Although corpses change during the decomposition process, the dead woman is not a replica of Diane. Her face has a different physiognomy. Perhaps Diane is dreaming in the last hope that all this is happening to someone else. The image of the dead woman becomes Diane in stages as she wakes up: first, we see her alive in dark clothing, then in dark clothing in the process of decomposition, and finally, she is wearing Diane's light-colored nightgown. Then

Diane wakes up and arrives in the present reality.

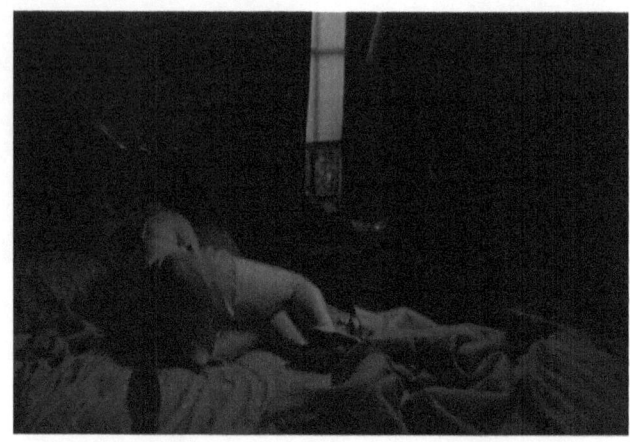

Is Diane asleep?

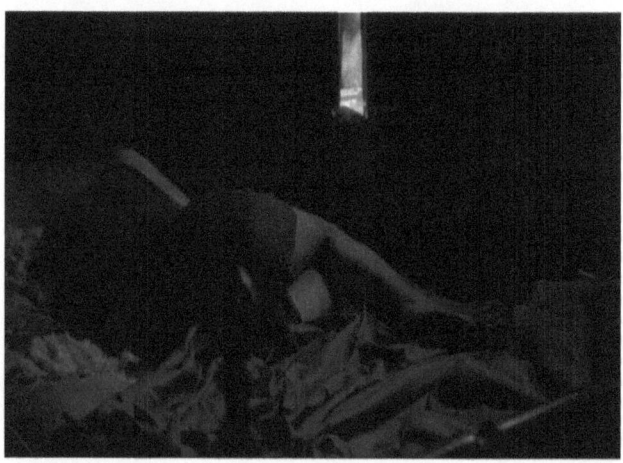

Is Diane dead?

AN EERILY ROMANTIC ENDING

Lynch's clue no. 7: What is felt, observed and gained in Club Silencio?

David Lynch was a romantic. He loved Gothic Romanticism, an undercurrent of Romanticism as defined by Edgar Allan Poe and, in Germany, E.T.A. Hoffmann. The central themes of Gothic Romanticism are curiosity, illusion, magic, sensory deception, imagination, the supernatural, and madness. All of these motifs can be found in Club Silencio. Lynch even takes up the doppelganger motif, a frequent element of Gothic romance, by visually aligning Betty and Rita with the blonde wig.

Betty and Rita spend their first night of love in bed together. At two o'clock in the morning, Rita wakes up with the words "Silencio" and "No hay banda" ("There is no band."). She anticipates the "key" scene that follows and introduces it.

David Lynch now leads us into the blue. Even during Betty and Rita's drive to Club Silencio, the lights in the surrounding houses, street lamps, and car headlights shimmer blue. The color, a central motif of the Romantic literary era, plays a significant role throughout the film. Blue stands for longing and the pursuit of knowledge and meaningfulness. In Romanticism, blue is a symbol of something that cannot be grasped rationally. To satisfy this longing, the unattainable must be achieved, even if this causes fear. This is particularly evident in the motif of the blue flower, a typical symbol of Romanticism. Lynch shows us blue flowers during the conversation between Betty and Rita at Winkie's. Such blue roses only exist in the dream in which the two find themselves.

The lettering and the front door of Club Silencio appear in shades of blue. The magic wand and the shirt of the performing magician (Richard Green) also glow blue. Betty learns from the mad magician on stage that she is an illusion. He explains this in three languages: in Spanish ("No hay banda!" - "There is no band."), In French ("Il n'y a pas d'orchestre." - "There is no orchestra.") and in English ("And yet, we hear a band." - "And yet we hear a band."). He speaks in all the languages that Diane mentions: English and French, her native languages from Canada, and Spanish through her relationship with Camilla.

A conductor leads an orchestra. If the conductor drops out, the orchestra can no longer play. Diane is the conductor of her dream - when she wakes up, the dream ends.

The magician explains to the dreaming Diane that she is hallucinating, that her mind has clouded her senses, and that she is not in reality. He conjures up a thunderstorm: there is thunder, blue lightning flashes, and Betty begins to tense up and tremble - the truth is shaking her. What resembles an epileptic seizure for Betty is

Diane's convulsive attempt not to wake up. She realizes that she is dreaming, but does not want to face reality.

The magician disappears in a cloud of blue smoke and gives Diane the chance to say goodbye. Diane's former landlord, Cookie, who may have a part-time job in the theater, announces the singer. The music of Hispanic singer Rebekah Del Rio, who performs the cover song "Llorando" (originally "Crying" by Roy Orbison), creates a melancholic atmosphere. Rita wears black, Betty red. Del Rio wears black and red - she is a part of Diane and a part of Camilla. Diane is allowed to mourn at this moment.

Rita and Betty weep bitterly, while Del Rio sings heartbreakingly:

Yo que pensé que te olvidé
pero es verdad, es la verdad
que te quiero aun más

mucho más que ayer
Dime tú que puedo hacer
¿No me quieres ya?
Y siempre estaré
llorando por tu amor
llorando por tu amor
Tu amor se llevó
todo mi corazón
Y quedo llorando, llorando, llorando, llorando
por tu amor.

Translation:
I thought I had forgotten you,
but it's true, so true,
that I still love you,
much more than yesterday.
Tell me, what can I do now?
Don't you love me anymore?
And I will always
cry for your love,

weep for your love.
Your love has taken my whole heart
and makes me weep, weep, weep
for your love.

Del Rio slumps as if dead, but the song continues. There is no more time to mourn. Diane knows that her relationship with Camilla is over for good and that the love between Betty and Rita was just an illusion. She must now wake up from the dream, face reality, and take the final step: kill herself.

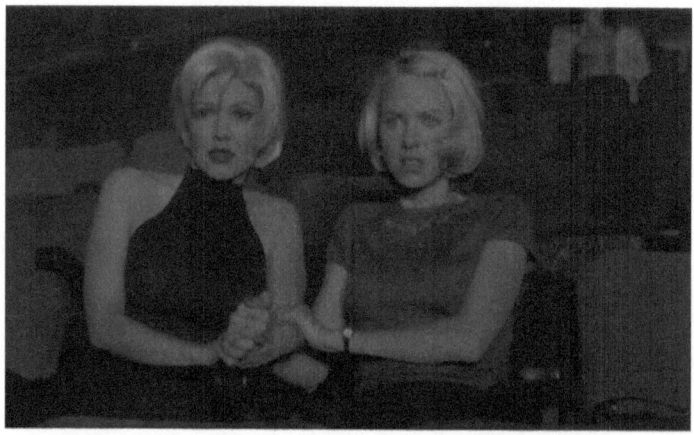

Fear and grief at Club Silencio

PANDORA'S BOX

Betty finds a box in her bag - an allusion to Pandora's box from Greek mythology, which contains the truth and reveals evil. The key to it is in Rita's bag in Aunt Ruth's apartment. Both dream figures leave the club and hurry to the apartment. Rita takes her bag and opens it. Betty immediately disappears because she is only a fiction of the dream. Rita calls for her, but she is no longer there. Rita opens the box, stares into the darkness, and the box falls to the floor.

Alea iacta est ("the die is cast") is a Latin expression from gambling and means "nothing works". The dreaming Diane sees her aunt Ruth, who seems to have heard that the box has fallen. Ruth enters the bedroom, looks at the floor, recognizes nothing, and leaves the room, shaking her head. Ruth can no longer do anything with what has happened because she has been dead for a long time. Diane realizes this at this moment. She wishes that Ruth were alive again, that she had never been in the apartment, and that the die had never been cast—but in vain.

Diane's dream ends when the knocking of her neighbor wakes her. When she is alone again, her flashbacks begin, and she remembers the actual events: Camilla ending the relationship on the couch, Diane masturbating in despair, remembering the party at Adam's, the humiliation at rehearsals, and the murder-for-hire conversation at Winkie's.

Her panic increases immeasurably when there is another knock at the door. Diane knows that the detectives are at the door looking for her as the murderer or the client. She hallucinates that her grandparents are crawling out from under the doorstep in miniature. They are chasing Diane to her death. Diane has let them down, hasn't made it in Hollywood. Driven by panic, she runs into her bedroom, pulls her gun out of the drawer, and shoots herself.

At first, it appears to be a murder in the heat of the moment, but in the overall context of the story, it becomes clear that Diane had already planned her death. She had probably bought the gun for this very moment. Her decision to die was made much earlier, after the relationship ended and Camilla's humiliation.

In the last scenes of the movie, we see a beautiful, radiant moment between Betty and Rita. Perhaps Diane sees this moment herself. Maybe she is allowed to be happy with her Camilla or as Betty with Camilla after her death. This may be decided by the woman with the blue hair who announces at the end: "Silencio!"

Is she an angel? Is she the waiting Aunt Ruth? Think, think some more!

A WACKY SHOOT BEHIND A WACKY STORY

An equally unusual origin story accompanies the extraordinary story of Mulholland Drive. David Lynch developed his first ideas for the subject back in 1990, initially in the context of a planned third season of *Twin Peaks*, set in Hollywood. However, he abandoned this plan in favor of other projects.

In February 1999, the Mulholland Drive series project finally took shape. ABC commissions Lynch to produce a pilot film, which is to serve as the basis for a ten-part series. But after viewing the 125-minute movie, which was made in just six weeks, ABC is horrified. Flimsy reasons were given: the leading actresses Naomi Watts and Laura Elena Harring were too old, there was too much smoking, and dog excrement appeared in the film. Lynch is stunned and is forced to shorten the pilot to 94 minutes.

Despite initial hopes, a final review by ABC leads to the definitive rejection of the project. Both the film and the planned series have been canceled. The official reason given was a lack of suspense and a narrative style that was too slow, which would not appeal to the television audience. This decision comes as a surprise to David Lynch and the actors involved. However, rumors are circulating behind the scenes that ABC is hesitant to portray Hollywood in an unfavorable light.

ABC is doing David Lynch an injustice, because the director loves Hollywood - he lives from it and for it. *Mulholland Drive* is thoroughly inspired by the American film industry and peppered with affectionate allusions to successful productions and famous actors. Even though Lynch highlights the darker side of Hollywood in his film, it is by no means his intention to harm the city. Rather, he lends it authenticity.

Hollywood is primarily known in the media as a place of glitz and glamor, where dreams are created and the best entertainment is produced. But behind this façade lies a tough business, characterized by money, power, intrigue, and suffering. *Mulholland Drive* tells the story of the many people who come to Hollywood with grand illusions and fail. Lynch shows the entire spectrum of life in the dream factory, from simple restaurant waiters to beggars. For some, Hollywood is heaven; for others, it is hell. Lynch condenses this ambivalence in the scene where Rita and Betty are driving to Club Silencio, as the camera pans past a street sign with the slogan "Hollywood is Hell." Likely, Lynch is also processing his nightmares in the film, which are also reflected in the rejection of his planned series. Thus, Adam's dream fate, as conceived by Diane, symbolizes the pressure and corrupt machinations in the American film industry. The director has no free choice and loses control over the cast, ultimately losing control over his movie.

The production of *Mulholland Drive* also threatens to turn into hell for Lynch due to ABC's rejection. But a year and a half later, Studio Canal Plus, a French production studio, is founded, which sees potential in the pilot. However, the studio did not want a series pilot, but a feature-length movie. Lynch gratefully accepts the challenge and sets about creating a self-contained feature film from the material. In doing so, he is faced with the task of resolving possible open storylines that would only have been resolved in the course of a potential series. Lynch solves this task in his unique way: He closes the storylines without actually resolving them.

This approach, which leaves the audience with numerous possible interpretations, is characteristic of Lynch's work and underscores his genius as a filmmaker. In this way, the original series plans are transformed into a cult film that still captivates numerous viewers today and encourages them to speculate about the story's meaning.

All the sets on which the original TV pilot was filmed have since been destroyed, costumes are no longer available, and actors are working on other films. A huge challenge for Lynch is that he uses material that has already been completed for the movie production. He had an additional 27 minutes filmed. The result is a 147-minute movie. The first two-thirds largely correspond to the original pilot, which ends with Rita opening the blue box and Betty disappearing. Some scenes are shortened for the feature film, others are added. New scenes include Diane's awakening, the visit from her neighbor, all the flashbacks to her real past (the pool party, Adam and Camilla at the shoot, the job interview at Winkie's), and Diane's suicide.

The opening scenes with the jitterbug dance competition and Diane's fall into bed are also new.

Anyone who claims that all of this is randomly thrown together and makes no sense fails to recognize Lynch's genius. He condenses a series and its secrets into 147 minutes, merely giving the audience clues to decipher them, hidden down to the smallest detail. Interviews suggest that the planned series would also have explored the dreams of various characters, in the tradition of Twin Peaks, and provided an open, interpretable ending.

REFERENCES IN AND CURIOSITIES ABOUT MULHOLLAND DRIVE

Mulholland Drive is rich in allusions, hidden clues, and fascinating backgrounds. In conclusion, the following alphabetically ordered list provides insight into additional references and interesting details surrounding the film that are not discussed in the main section. It includes direct references to other works of film and cultural history as well as surprising facts about the making and reception of the film. This collection is designed to help readers better understand the depth and complexity of Lynch's masterpiece, while providing entertaining insights into the world behind the scenes.

Angelo Badalamenti

Film composer Angelo Badalamenti, who created the incomparable soundtrack for

Mulholland Drive, also plays the character Luigi Castigliane in the film. Angelo Badalamenti. This is not his first appearance in a Lynch film. He already had a small role as a bar pianist in *Blue Velvet*.

Addresses

When the cab driver asks the dream Betty where he should take her, she replies, "1612 Havenhurst." Havenhurst Drive is located in West Hollywood, but the highest house number there is 1477. The famous Sunset Boulevard, where the first film studio was built in 1910, crosses at the end of the street. No other street is as synonymous with Hollywood glitz and glamor. The Chateau Marmont Hotel, situated directly at the intersection of Havenhurst Drive and Sunset Boulevard, is considered the most famous short-term or long-term residence of prominent personalities from the film industry.

The "1612 Havenhurst" apartment complex is reminiscent of this famous address. If Havenhurst Drive were longer, the Chateau Marmont could bear the house number 1612.

This visual reference was certainly not incorporated into the film by David Lynch by chance. The director is known for using fictitious addresses. Adam Kesher's villa at "6980 Mulholland Drive" does not exist in reality either. If it were in the given location, it would be situated right next to the Jerome C. Daniel Overlook parking lot, offering a view of the Hollywood sign, the Hollywood Bowl, and the city of Los Angeles.

The Sierra Bonita facility featured in the film is located in Silver Lake, a neighborhood of Los Angeles, rather than in Hollywood itself. The real plant inspired David Lynch.

Alfred Hitchcock

Mulholland Drive is rich in allusions to Alfred Hitchcock's *Vertigo*, which enrich the film's structure and atmosphere. Visually, this becomes clear when Betty covers Rita's mouth in one scene, which is strongly reminiscent of Scott's similar gesture to Judy/Madeleine in *Vertigo*. The use of striking color schemes that create a dreamlike mood is also a parallel to Hitchcock's work. Thematically, both films share a fascination with doppelgangers, changing identities, and the obsession with being someone else. The transformation of characters, often by changing their hair color, is another unifying element. Narratively, Lynch, like Hitchcock, uses a non-linear narrative style that revolves around traumatic events and blurs the boundaries between reality, dream, and fantasy. In addition, both directors use voyeuristic elements and subjective camerawork to put the audience in the perspective of the characters. These diverse references demonstrate how Lynch incorporates Hitchcock's cinematic devices and themes into his unmistakable style to tell a multi-layered and complex story.

Car accident

Laura Elena Harring experienced an eerie premonition the day before her audition for *Mulholland Drive*. On the way to the audition for the role of Camilla/Rita, she was involved in a car accident, unaware that this incident would later play a central role in her film character. At the audition, Harring told casting agent Johanna Ray about the accident, whereupon she asked in surprise whether she had read the script, as her character had a car accident in the opening scene. Both recognized the bizarre coincidence. Harring herself saw it as a sign from the universe that she was in the right place. Interestingly,

Lynch had previously chosen Harring for the role based on a photograph. This incident highlights the often-discussed fusion of reality and fiction in Lynch's work, illustrating how random events seem to correspond with art in an uncanny manner—a theme that also plays a significant role in *Mulholland Drive*.

Bathrobe

The pink bathrobe that Naomi Watts wears during her audition in *Mulholland Drive* also appears in David Lynch's short film *Rabbits* (2002), which was shot shortly after the release of *Mulholland Drive*. In addition to Watts, Laura Elena Harring and Scott Coffey also appear in *Rabbits*, which underlines the connection between the two works. Like *Mulholland Drive*, *Rabbits* is characterized by a surreal and unsettling atmosphere.

Resident sign

The name of Diane's neighbor (played by Johanna Stein) could be "L. J. DeRosa". It is written on the resident's sign in the Sierra Bonita complex, next to apartment no. 17. In the end credits, we learn that Laura J. DeRosa was a crew member of the film; she is listed there as a "construction buyer."

Billy Wilder

Mulholland Drive is peppered with allusions to Billy Wilder's *Sunset Boulevard*. In one scene, for example, Lynch's camera specifically focuses on a street sign that reads *"Sunset Blvd." and uses the same car model (Isotta-Fraschini) from the late 1920s that can also be seen in the film "Sunset Boulevard."*

Edward Hopper

Edward Hopper, a renowned American realist painter whose works often explore the loneliness and alienation of modern life, was a significant influence on David Lynch's filmmaking. In Mulholland, there are clear allusions to Hopper's painting style, characterized by muted colors, gloomy lighting, and sober American realism. The depiction of isolation and ambiguity, as well as the minimalist decor and the reduced landscape narratives, are also inspired by Hopper. This blurs the boundaries between reality and dream, creating an unsettling yet fascinating atmosphere reminiscent of Hopper's paintings.

The monster behind Winkie's ...

The sinister "monster" in *Mulholland Drive* is embodied by actress Bonnie Aarons, whose striking facial features and striking green eyes already impressed Lynch at a *Twin Peaks party*. The fact that a woman plays the "monster" supports the interpretation that it represents Diane's inner demons, feelings of guilt, and her perception of herself as a "monster". The character's green eyes are often interpreted as a metaphor for jealousy, a central theme in Diane's story. Lynch took great care to ensure that Aaron's eyes were visible in the scene, emphasizing the importance of gaze and perception in the film. The scene was shot so that Aaron was looking directly into the camera, where Lynch himself was standing, giving the moment a particular intensity and immediacy. The casting of a woman is another example of Lynch's play with identity and perception, and underlines the multi-layered interpretative possibilities of the film as well as the complex psychology of the main character, Diane Selwyn.

The Wizard of Oz

David Lynch has a deep fascination with *The Wizard of Oz* (1939), which manifests itself in many ways in his films. The restaurant Winkie's, for example, is an allusion to the Winkies from the Land of Oz. The color yellow, which plays an important role in *Oz* - think of the yellow brick road - can also be found in Lynch's work, for example, in the yellow cab that introduces Betty's dream journey in *Mulholland Drive*. Both *Oz* and Lynch's films thematize the blurring of reality and dream and the protagonist's journey through a strange, often threatening world. Visual references can be found in *Wild at Heart*, where Sheryl Lee appears as Glinda, the good witch. The use of curtains, especially red ones, in Lynch's films could also be inspired by the Wizard's revelation in *Oz*. The color palette of blue, red, yellow, and black that Lynch frequently uses carries symbolic meaning. In *Mulholland Drive*, the characters Coco and Aunt Ruth could be allusions to characters from the Oz books, specifically Aunt Em. Similar to *Oz*, Lynch's films often feature characters who are introduced in real life and then reinterpreted in a dream world. Lynch himself has stated that he thinks about *The Wizard of Oz* every day, which underscores the profound and lasting impact the film has had on his work. This connection was even explored in depth in the documentary *Lynch/Oz* (2022).

Jack Nicholson

Adam Kesher's outburst of rage, in which he smashes the windshield of the Castigliane brothers' car with a golf club, is a reference to

Jack Nicholson. In 1994, Nicholson lost his nerve in heavy traffic, got out of his car, and smashed the windshield of another road user in a rage. Nicholson was subsequently charged with damage to property and assault. However, the case was settled out of court after the actor apologized and paid an undisclosed sum to Blank. In later interviews, Nicholson described the incident as " a shameful incident in my life" and explained that great stress caused by the death of a close friend and the pressure of filming had led to his outburst. Incidentally, Nicholson's nickname is " Mulholland Man ". This goes back to his role in Roman Polanski's film *Chinatown,* in which he plays a fictionalized William Mulholland, after whom the street is named. Interestingly, Nicholson himself has lived on Mulholland Drive for many years.

Jean-Luc Godard

Mulholland Drive has several parallels with Jean-Luc Godard's *Contempt* (1963). Not only is the name of the main character, Camille (Brigitte Bardot), and her red bathrobe similar, but the color palette of both films is also strongly dominated by red and blue. In addition, both works focus on a director who is forced to make compromises in his work and end with the word "Silencio". A scene in a sparsely populated theater plays an important role in both films. In both *Contempt* and *Mulholland Drive*, there are scenes of failing electricity, a motif Lynch also uses in other films. Camille *in Contempt* puts on a dark wig and looks at herself in the mirror, while Rita in *Mulholland Drive* puts on a blonde wig. Both films address the problems of film production and the pressure on directors to compromise, and feature scenes of characters getting into vintage convertibles. Both works conclude with scenes that address filmmaking itself, and the "silencio" at the end of both films can be understood as a commentary on the artificiality of the film medium. Both *Contempt* and *Mulholland Drive* are self-reflexive works that critically examine filmmaking and the film industry, and both directors use multilingual elements to emphasize the international nature of the film industry.

Justin Theroux

Justin Theroux took the cowboy's threat ("You'll see me again if you do it right. You'll see me twice more if you do it wrong.") obviously very seriously. As he didn't receive the entire script at once, he asked David Lynch several times how many more times his character, Adam, would see the cowboy. Lynch's answer: " I don't know. We have to find out together.

Art

Mulholland Drive is far more than a cinematic masterpiece - it's a visual journey through the eras of art history. Especially in Adam's house, which serves as a mirror image of modern Hollywood, Lynch interweaves subtle allusions to classical and contemporary art.

For example, there is a highly symbolic replica of Guido Reni's famous 16th-century painting, Beatrice Cenci. Next to it hangs another painting that is reminiscent of *Our Lady of Guadalupe* - also from the 16th century. This work refers not only to religious motifs but also to the cultural and spiritual roots of many immigrants in the United States.

In contrast, Aunt Ruth's House, reminiscent of the golden age of Hollywood, houses a collection of classical-style artwork. This juxtaposition of old and new is emphasized by an abstract painting in Adam's house, which provides a clear contrast to the classical and modern works in Aunt Ruth's house. The different art styles in the two houses thus reflect the various eras of Hollywood and illustrate how the city has changed over time.

Head to the cinema on set

Like the audience, the actors were also in the dark and had many questions for the director during the shoot. However, Lynch refused to explain the true meaning of the movie to them. He answered their questions in code, but did not give any direct answers.

Mr. Roque

Michael J. Anderson, who plays Mr. Roque,

suffers from the genetic disorder osteogenesis imperfecta, also known as brittle bone disease. He is only 1.09 meters tall. For his role, Anderson was fitted with a prosthesis to make him appear taller. Andersen also plays the mysterious dwarf in *Twin Peaks*.

Dedication

David Lynch dedicated *Mulholland Drive* to actress Jennifer Maria Syme, who had already appeared in his film *Lost Highway*. Syme, who started as an intern for Lynch at the age of 16 and worked for his production company for five years, had a significant influence on the music in his films, especially the soundtrack of *Lost Highway*. She also made a small appearance in this film as "Junkie Girl". Tragically, Syme died in a car accident in 2001. Lynch was deeply affected by her death and carried the coffin at her funeral. The dedication from *Mulholland Drive* in the film's end credits is a poignant tribute to the young woman whose life ended tragically and who had a profound influence on Lynch's work.

William Mulholland

The namesake of Mulholland Drive was an important hydraulic engineer. At the beginning of the 20th century, William Mulholland organized the city's drinking water supply, making a decisive contribution to its growth.

PRODUCTION NOTES

Original title: Mulholland Drive
German title: Mulholland Drive - Road to Darkness
Director: David Lynch
Writer: David Lynch
Producers: Pierre Edelman, Neal Edelstein, Joyce Eliason, Tony Krantz, Michael Polaire, Alain Sarde, Mary Sweeney, John Wentworth
Production location: USA, France 2000
Studios: Asymmetrical Productions, Imagine Television, Le Studio Canal +, Les Film Alain Sarde, The Picture Factory, Touchstone Television
Distribution: Universal Pictures
Cinematography: Peter Dening
Music: Angelo Badalamenti

Editing: Mary Sweeny
Costume: Amy Stofsky
Technique: 33 mm, color
Budget: 15 million dollars
Box office: 20,112,339 dollars
Running time: 147 minutes
World premiere: 16.05.2001 (Cannes)
US theatrical release: 12.10.2001
German release: 03.01.2002
Video release Germany: 11.07.2002
MPAA: rated R for violence, language, and some strong sexuality
FSK: 16 years
Awards:
Cannes International Film Festival 2001
- Best Director: David Lynch (Palme d'Or)
Los Angeles Film Critics Association 2001
Best Director (David Lynch)
- 2nd place: Best Film

- 2nd place: Best Actress (Naomi Watts)

Chlotrudis Awards 2002

- Best movie
- Best Director (David Lynch)
- Best Screenplay (David Lynch)
- Best Actress (Naomi Watts)
- Best Screenplay Audience Award (David Lynch)

Full Cast

Naomi Watts - Diane Selwyn

Naomi Watts - Betty Elms

Laura Elena Harring - Camilla Rhodes

Laura Elena Harring - Rita

Justin Theroux - Adam Kesher

Robert Forster - Detective Harry McKnight

Brent Briscoe - Detective Domgaard

Ann Miller - Coco Lenoix

Ann Miller - Coco Kesher
Dan Hedaya - Vincenzo Castigliane
Mark Pellegrino - Joe
Jeanne Bates - Irene
Dan Birnbaum - Irene's Companion
Scott Wulff - Limo Driver
Maya Bond - Aunt Ruth
Patrick Fischler - Dan
Michael Cooke - Herb
Bonnie Aarons - Bum
Michael J. Anderson - Mr. Roque
Joseph Kearney - Roque's Manservant
Enrique Buelna - Back of Head Man
Richard Mead - Hairy-Armed Man
Sean E. Markland - Cab Driver at LAX
Angelo Badalamenti - Luigi Castiglianne
David Schroeder - Robert Smith
Robert Katims - Ray Hott

Marcus Graham - Mr. Darby
Tom Morris - Espresso Man
Melissa George - Camilla Rhodes
Mo Gallini - Castiglianne Limo Driver
Vincent Castellanos - Ed
Diane Nelson - Heavy-Set Woman
Charles Croughwell - Vacuum Man
Rena Riffel - Laney
Michael Des Barres - Billy
Lori Heuring - Lorraine
Billy Ray Cyrus - Gene
Tad Horino - Taka
Melissa Crider - Waitress at *Winkie's*
Tony Longo - Kenny
Daniel Rey - Valet Attendant
Geno Silva - Hotel Manager
Geno Silva - Emcee
Katharine Towne - Cynthia

Lee Grant - Louise Bonner
Monty Montgomery - The Cowboy
Kate Forster - Martha Johnson
James Karen - Wally Brown
Chad Everett - Jimmy Katz
Wayne Grace - Bob Brooker
Rita Taggart - Linny James
Michele Hicks - Nicki
Lisa Ferguson - 1st AC
William Ostrander - 2nd Assistant Director
Elizabeth Lackey - Carol
Brian Beacock - Backup Singer No. 1
Blake Lindsley - Backup Singer No. 2
Adrien Curry - Backup Singer No 3
Tyrah M. Lindsey - Backup Singer No. 4
Michael Weatherred -Hank--
Michael Fairman - Jason
Johanna Stein - Woman in No. 12

Richard Green - The Magician
Conti Condoli - Trumpet Player
Cori Glazer - Blue-Haired Lady
Rebekah Del Rio - Herself
Lyssie Powell - Blonde in Bed
Scott Coffey - Wilkins
Kimberly Clever - Dancer
Joshua Collazo - Dancer
Lisa Ferguson - Dancer
David Frutos - Dancer
Peter Loggins - Dancer
Theresa Salazar - Dancer
Thea Samuels - Dancer
Christian Thompson - Dancer
Justin Theroux - Adam Kesher
Naomi Watts - Betty Elms
Laura Elena Harring - Rita
Ann Miller - Coco Lenoix

Dan Hedaya - Vincenzo Castigliane
Mark Pellegrino - Joe
Robert Forster - Det. Harry McKnight
Katharine Towne - Cynthia Jenzen
Lee Grant - Louise Bonner
Michael J. Anderson - Mr. Roque
Diane Baker
Scott Coffey - Wilkins
Billy Ray Cyrus - Gene
Chad Everett - Jimmy Katz
Melissa George - Camilla Rhodes
Marcus Graham - Vincent Darby
Sean E. Markland
Monty Montgomery - Cowboy
James Karen - Casting Director

FILMOGRAPHY

Feature films
Inland Empire (2006)
Mulholland Drive (2001)
The Straight Story (1999)
Lost Highway (1997)
Twin Peaks: Fire Walk with Me (1992)
Wild at Heart (1990)
Blue Velvet (1986)
Dune (1984)
The Elephant Man (1980)
Eraserhead (1977)

Short films and experiments
More Things That Happened (2007)
Boat (2007)
The Three Rs (2011)
Lady Blue Shanghai (2010)

Darkened Room (2002)
Industrial Symphony No. 1 (1990)
The Cowboy and the Frenchman (1988)
The Amputee (1974)
The Grandmother (1970)
The Alphabet (1968)
Six Figures Getting Sick (1966)
TV series and episodes
Twin Peaks: The Return (2017)
Hotel Room (1993)
On the Air (1992)
Twin Peaks (1990-1991)
American Chronicles (1990)

Other film projects
Lumière et compagnie (1995) - contribution to the omnibus film

| Les Français vus par (1988) - contribution to the TV series |

The End

www.ingramcontent.com/pod-product-compliance
Lightning Source LLC
Chambersburg PA
CBHW030653220526
45463CB00005B/1755